DRAW SPACES

Maisie Nesbitt

Now I Know My ABCs

© 2021 **Europe Books** | London
www.europebooks.co.uk – info@europebooks.co.uk

ISBN 979-12-201-1007-5
First edition: August 2021

Now I Know My ABCs

"A teacher thought I was smarter than I was, so I was."

To all the children who allowed me to put the Pygmalion effect into action; may they grow to be freely-shaped adults.

To my family, my partner and my close friends who believed in this book when I didn't.

To the teachers I have seen in action, who in their turn, shaped me.

Foreword

Who doesn't have memories of the early (and the latest) days of school? Are there any memories in a person's life remembered more bittersweetly than those of the days spent in the classroom and behind a school desk? One's identity begins to form and discover itself in those days, without the awareness of it happening. It is with irony, care, patience, and above all with a particular and heartfelt tenderness shining through the pages of her poetry collection that Maisie Nesbitt writes about her pupils and her experience in teaching to the youngest. A task that, unfortunately, is made much harder by the severe but essential safety norms dictated by the COVID-19 pandemic. Whilst being kept as safe as possible, the young students lose the possibility of learning through the spontaneous social interactions that usually take place in the classroom, and they involuntarily miss an important step in their social skills development – a step that can surely be recovered, but not without time, perseverance, and dedication from the combined efforts of the child, teacher, and parents. An online learning timetable is what they are left with; that, and the patience of an attentive teacher that can just about try to mitigate the effect that a cold, impersonal screen can have on children's attention during the lessons and its impact on their daily lives. And that very screen can sometimes reveal insecurities and exacerbate loneliness. But 'The Virus', as it is addressed in the poems, was followed by something unexpectedly wonderful from the children's families. The lockdown and the atmosphere of emergency brought out the families' support and understanding towards the teachers and all those working in education, and without this empathy going through the pandemic would be so much harder; the proof that, in adversities, a united front is vital.

Teaching to children is a vocation rather than a job; it's a personal quest composed of small moments in time, moments that apparently can seem meaningless, repetitive, and unchanging, such as sharpening a pencil, marking a spelling mistake, receiving what at times can seem like endless complaints or unrequested advice from the parents... But being an educator is much more than that. What for an adult is nothing but a fleeting moment, for a child is a formative memory that will grow as the child grows, developing a unique character, shaped and molded not only by the teachings that have been received but also according to the experiences that have been made. The educator knows that the acts of teaching and learning are experiences themselves and as such will be remembered, ingrained, and encased in the child's memory. Educating is taking a child's hand and walking together, ready to let go at the right moment, when the reassuring, guiding presence is no longer needed and another chapter of the story is about to be told. So, every small gesture becomes a ritual, and every seemingly meaningless ritual has its significance, its weight in the path of a young, developing mind. With time, as the class grows faster than what seems possible, learns, gathers independence and self-confidence, so grows the teacher, whose pupils act, in a way, like a mirror: as you change and shape them, they change and shape you; as they grow and transition to a different stage in education, you find yourself growing and discover that, in a way, somehow, they managed to stay with you.

Now I know my ABCs

Assessments you photocopy-count-mark-moderate-remark-report-summarise on loop,
Book scrutiny leading to the realisation of an underperforming class,
Call-over meeting, "Could try harder, his inference is not up to scratch,"
Demonstrating progress is a slogan engraved in your brain,
E-mail from parent listing your shortcomings when you tried to
Fix and patch minor playground spats
Guaranteed to make you question your sense of justice.
How can I reach out to that particular child?
Interest you consistently try to spark, keep ablaze and sustain,
Justifying actions, words and grades whilst persistently
Kicking yourself because you forgot to introduce-explain-evaluate,
Leaving on a Friday with shoulders a little less slumped
Monday comes round so soon, only for muscular and mental tension to return
Not giving you respite until the following weekend.
Obtaining the absolute best from twenty-two children when worrying you, as one, have conveyed your worst.
Pressure from all sides to deliver-stretch-challenge even when
Questions are pitched to all levels, scaffolded, repeated and stimulated but met with silence.
Relaxation is a sense mixed and blended with guilt;
So much more I should be doing, you think, and yet
Too little time, always.
Until every full stop is correctly placed I will relentlessly repeat myself

Vehemently though unconsciously adopting catchphrases from your own childhood like,
"Walk, children, don't run – how many more times do I need to say it?"
X-country races you witness and quell meltdowns in;
You eventually train yourself to praise and reprimand using only your eyes,
Zipping mouths shut as your own has to be when asked once more to change what you do.

Well, now I know my ABCs.
I wished I had been warned school would entail all this for me.

Close Encounters of the After School Kind

It tends to happen at the local supermarket
Between 5 and 6 in the evening
Where a fascinated voice calls out your name.
"Hiiiiiiiiiiiiiiii, Miss!"
"Are you buying that pizza?"
"Is this your boyfriend?"
"Look, Mummy, it's my teacher!"
You wave back and smile demurely when you are
Caught out.
Admittedly, you have dodged certain voices, backs of heads
And whole families,
Hoping to remain in a safe shopping trolley bubble
Stocking up on wine, crisps and tampons
After a day spent by your trusted whiteboard.

Never Enough

Sometimes I sing the song from *The Greatest Showman*
And change the words to replicate
my feelings and frustrations.
All the praise from a thousand lessons
All the hours that I spend marking books will
Never be enough, never be enough
Towers of plans are still too little
This brain could differentiate the world but it'll
Never be enough, never be enough… for some.
It is a minority, of that I am aware
Who complain, nag, insist and insidiously judge
But it is enough to demean, crush, and overturn my work.
Hot-embered complaints sent online with vehemence,
Brusque words uttered before the chance to begin or end my day,
Misinterpretations of a written mark or spoken reprimand
Are enough to make me feel I
Will never be enough… for some… or for me.

Ones of Your Own

There are inevitable times
When you hear something funny,
See a twinkling, inspired eye
Or receive a meaningful hug
Where you do think of ones of your own.
What would they be called?
How would they reach for your hand?
What colour baby-grows and bibs would you dress them in?
Then there are other times
When you see tears, tantrums, snot and vomit,
Hear stubbornness or just plain defiance
And spend a particular type of lesson
Frustrated and unheard,
Where you think of anything but having
Ones of your own.

Fleeing the Nest

Fed with warm porridge, buttery toast
Or colourful cereal,
Feathers washed, tidied and dressed in a new uniform,
Bodies prepped by turning pages in picture books and by holding felt tips,
Your young wings are ready to spread and fly.
September is the time to flee the nest,
Choose a seat, make new friends.
A time to trust new teachers,
To open their mind,
To travel on their own
To warmer, unknown, exciting climes.

Learning Curves

Flattening and rising like roller coasters
are the learning curves of all practitioners
who never stop facing new subjects and themes,
new rules,
new technologies,
new pupils and their unique needs
(I say unique and not 'special' as an aside because somehow our society has assigned to that adjective some negative, inferior connotations. As if being 'special' could ever be undesirable).
Falling and dropping like surfers' waves
are our fields of expertise and ignorance,
our own sense first of competence and then, overwhelming lack of knowledge.
How can I teach this?
How can I improve that?
Why was that lesson simply full of rubbish?
Learning curves, up and down, much like attending school all over again.
How ironic.

Assembly

Rows of cross-legged children,
Hymn books at hand,
Sitting (more or less) quietly, awaiting for the start.
"Good morning, everybody," the ingrained, lulling chant
As the headmaster begins his weekly announcements
Of sports matches, Parents Evenings, upcoming events,
Reminding, asking, praising, addressing.
Then, all stand as one
For the school song.
"How daft," you used to think,
"Although miles better than heavily religious ones."
"How passionate," you now think,
As the hall rings with the chorus sung in unison.
It's just your school song.
It would mean nothing to anybody else.
But to you, now, it is starting to sum up all you stand for.
All your values.
"Don't be daft now," you then think
But smile knowingly at yourself.

Another Year Over

It is not in December that teachers reminisce,
Make resolutions
And reflect on the new year ahead,
But in the summer.
July, another year over, perhaps a new classroom,
Always a new cohort
To replace your pupils who looked far too young just last September
And are now destined for greater things than your own four display-boarded walls.
You have learned of their favourite foods, animals, songs and subjects;
You have laughed with them and silenced them;
You have been bursting with pride and trembling with frustration
In all functions, events and daily aspects of life here.
As the sun beats down warmly, you wipe the slate clean
And already start wondering
About new register orders, labels, names, quirks and habits
Another Year Over,
A new one to begin in the Autumn Term.

Miss Honey and Miss Trunchbull

Inexperienced and naïve, you start your first day,
Your pale madonna face which Roald Dahl described
Breaks into a smile despite your insecurities.
And just like that, the children take to you.
They smile back, laugh, learn and progress;
They leave cards, tokens, gifts on your desk;
Their tasks begin to take form.
Their intellects begin to sprout new leaves.

Then comes Ms Trunchbull,
Marching like a storm-trooper,
Red-faced, booming voice,
Crashing, shouting, slamming, staring.
And so you doubt whether children have taken to you after all,
Whether you can reach their ears, brains and hearts after all,
But then you remember how *Matilda* ends;
Which teacher runs away screaming and frightened
And which one discovers hidden talents and powers.

Parents Evening Jousting

You gather your books as darkness descends,
Mark book as your noble steed,
Compliments and anecdotes as your shining armour,
Advice, Next Steps forward and targets strengthen your shield.

The hall is crowded as you take your place
Facing your opponents,
Who have chosen a five-minute slot via the School Office
For the privilege of this jousting.

You have steeled yourself for these duels;
You step back and charge
Replies like jabs to your head and chest,
You retreat, rephrase, repeat.

The Parents Evening Jousting
A popular yet risky event
As it produces several wounds
Occasionally patched by the plaster of a 'thank you'.

Pastoral Care

A pastor, or a shepherd
Guides his flocks through fields to graze,
Ensuring their safe return before the fall of darkness.
No term could be more apt for the care we give
To our flock of 22, 13 or 30-odd,
Guiding them through classrooms to learn,
Ensuring their safe return home at 4 pm.
We are shepherds through teary mornings
In which Mum or Dad were in a bad mood
Through arguments with classmates and siblings,
Past worries about assessments, exams, homework, lessons, clubs, team practices,
Divorces, separations, house moves, births, bereavements, redundancies, pay cuts,
Illnesses, surgeries, recoveries, counselling, new partners and spouses for parents,
Accidents, injuries, abuses and suspicions of,
Recurring nightmares, phobias, SEND needs and anxieties.
Pastors with our flock,
Lighthouses with our lost sailors
Guiding. Ensuring. Steering and propelling.

The Show Must Go On

Your whole class has been counting down the weeks and days,
Flyers have not escaped anybody's field of vision.
It is now here: The School Play.
You head to the theatre with a makeup kit assembled,
Certainly not Instagram-model-worthy, but it will do.
You wonder how your creativity will be tested this time round;
Is it sheep? Rabbits? Dinosaurs? Princesses? Foxes and zebras? Elderly villagers?
The buzzing queue by your workstation snakes through
Coils around the changing rooms and writhes by the costumes.
Each bright-eyed pupil fantasises about the Hollywood sign
And paparazzi flashes which no doubt will be in their destiny.
Boys a little sullen and itchy in their bow ties and foundation,
Girls a Shirley Temple invocation
Asking for mascara, eyebrows, bronzer (how do they even know what that is?)
You can't help but smile in reminiscence
Of your own experiences of school theatres.
Year in, year out, you know the children will be transformed,
Lines forgotten, dancers dropped or props misplaced.
The Show Must Go On
And every child on that stage,
Be it a chorus line or the protagonists,
Will shine unexpectedly
And ever brighter to their family's eyes.

Perspectives

"My child is absolutely acing his spellings,"
And then they write of a farst floeing rivor by a smll byutiful hows.
"My boy is polite, caring and friendly to all,"
And then you catch them snatching, pushing, name-calling and face-pulling.
"My girl can understand and interpret all the complicated books she reads,"
And then when you ask for her favourite chapter, character or plot event, she cannot give a precise, clear answer.
"Our children are absolutely terrified of your sanctions,"
And then they repeatedly, openly, defiantly challenge all boundaries and rules.
"My child's handwriting and comprehension are shocking,"
But then they produce sensitive, relevant, creative stories, un-read outside school.
"My boy just has no interest in reading at home,"
But then there is never time for them to listen, talk, ask, and sign a Reading Record.
"My girl is still not in the highest ability group,"
But then they have progressed furthest than you ever thought possible, with the right approach and support.
"Our children are absolutely terrified in your lessons,"
But then they turn up every morning with smiles, curiosity and carefully-completed homework.

It's all a matter of perspectives.

Technological Proximity

For all its advantages
Technology, social media and its readily-available nature
Mean that in most weekend and holidays there is no respite.

Just when you start getting used to being called by your first name at home
Rather than 'Miss', 'Mrs' or 'Sir'
You hear the dreaded ping from your device.

"We hope you have had a wonderful Christmas
But are worried about our darling son
Whose average seems to be a whole 1% below that of the year group."

"We wish you a Happy New Year
However we also wish you would attend to this matter
Involving our delightful daughter and the fallout she has had with a friend."

"We apologise for e-mailing you on a Sunday morning
With a request to discuss potential scholarships
And secondary schools to which our 7-year-old should apply."

The technological proximity created
Can be useful in most times and yet haunting in this context
Where you just wish for a brief escape from those four classroom walls.

The Largest Art Gallery in the World

I have seen Botticelli's works in Florence,
Magritte's at the Guggenheim,
Impressionist landscapes at the Musée D'Orsay.
However, if I owned the largest art gallery in the world,
I would fill it up with my pupils' artworks and cards.
I would populate its walls with doe-eyed, curly-lashed kittens,
Flowers, rainbows, teddy bears, emoji faces,
Halloween pumpkins, Christmas trees and snowflakes
And the most sincere, heartfelt messages of thanks
Written in wobbly gel pen.

Through Readers' Eyes

Scanning and scrutinising the page,
Deciphering and sounding out,
Labouring over letters, blends, digraphs and other such signs
Until the stammered sound like a scratched record
Then flows like a river escaping its lock,
m-a-t to mat to mathematics,
Whole paragraphs rush out of lips,
Entire stories drip, leak, gush, then flow with the currents
And as from mouth, soon from pencil,
Through readers' eyes the world will be written.
Through readers' eyes conversations will be understood.
Through readers' eyes relationship will be formed.

Leaving Their Mark

Poetically, I could say that learning to write allows my class to
Leave a mark for posterity,
Document their thoughts and experiences,
Portray what they imagine and perceive.
Realistically, I will say that teaching to write entails
Deciphering hieroglyphs which barely rest on the notebook's lines.
Maniacally sharpening pencils and presenting rubbers,
Pointing out at all the missing capital letters and full stops,
Marking pages and pages of streams of consciousness
Involving dragons and trolls and Fortnite dances and footballers,
When the prompt simply asked to 'Describe your bedroom'.
Optimistically, it means that there will be times where you spot
Magical elements and symbols on the page
Like a comma, or the adjectives notable and magnificent,
A full clearly-indented paragraph (Oh, the rarity of this…)
Or even a spontaneous simile.
Leaving their mark
For you to interpret,
Sometimes despair and massage your scalp,
Some other times, puzzle over, smile and chuckle.

Visitors to the Zoo

You had circled this date a few weeks ago
On your planner, in red,
Yearly Performance Review, focus on pupil-led learning.
That is the theme this time
and you have repeated it to yourself in an attempt to fall asleep.
The visitors will be there soon;
Their tickets, in the form of your lesson plans, are placed by the door,
The title is underlined on your whiteboard,
Your businesswoman blazer is ironed and donned.
But these visits do not often go to plan;
The lovable monkeys may play up, throw their bananas in tantrums,
Refuse to put their hands up as you have taught them insistently.
The dolphins may suddenly play dumb,
Forgetting all the key terminology, powerful words and creative thoughts,
Playing the act of pufferfish.
The cubs may turn into cheetahs,
Rushing through your tasks at the speed of light,
Leaving you with an empty, unplanned 20 minutes of this live show.
In this visit to the zoo you must think on your feet,
Trusting even the untamed animals to be showcased,
And when all is over and your armpits and palms are discreetly sweating
And the animals surround you for feeding time
Asking, "Who were those people at the back?"
You can breathe out, smile and reply, "No one to worry about, now."

Vitamin C

You may have hated what you saw in the mirror this morning,
You may have had a row with a loved one,
You may be feeling under the weather,
Or you may be facing and fighting a more serious ailment.
You may have received some unsettling news,
You may have had a spat with your neighbours,
Or you may have had a dreadful drive in standstill traffic.
You may have been rejected, criticised, insulted
Questioned, opposed, frowned upon.
But when those doors open
And those heads turn
And that chorus says, "Good morning," with your name loud and clear
And they ask you how you are
And they plead you for a story
And they say, "Thank you,"
And they say, "I get it now,"
That works better than any tonic or medicine,

Which is why you might be able to boost your immune system,
Against all the world's shittiest evils,
With some generously-dosed Vitamin C, generated in this Classroom.

Festive Outlook on Life

Although the Christmas build-up
Might bring angst, frustration, tongue-biting and fist-clenching,
Consumerism galore and a bout of misanthropy
There is nothing like a child's festive outlook on it all.

Advent calendars concealing creamy treasures,
Lists compiled in best, joined-up writing,
Cards with interpretations of holly, snowmen and reindeer,
Windows decked with misshapen flakes and chains.

The fervour with which carols are sung,
The eagerness with which sheep, shepherd and wise men perform on stages
Wearing Bethlehem garments with Clarks pumps and brogues,
The sheer belief of what they sing blatant in their eyes and cheeks.

Their festive outlook on December and on life
Thaws even the blackest, most Bah-Humbug of hearts
And we believe again once more
In finding something unexpected at the foot of a tree.

(Not) Fitting a Mould

The cards are laid on the table;
In other words, the books are laid out on the desk,
Crooked, misshapen handwriting,
Spellings as undecipherable as an MI6 code.
You try to gently, softly, politely, professionally
Underline the discrepancies,
The need for further investigation and support,
The need for time, thought and extra care
For a child that does not quite fit the mould.
Not quite quick enough on his feet,
Not really where he is supposed to be
According to the machines, rankings and systems that rule all this.
They think outside the box
So much that the box has lost its contours and they have no references,
No guidelines, no confines within which to work and understand.
You want to make that mould malleable
For that extraordinary child,
So that all the liquid matter of his creativity, energy and obstacles can be
Made solid again.
At times, the welders are understanding
Even grateful, emotional and relieved
At other times they riot
They insist that the mould fits, it fitted for them in the past and it
Must
Fit
Now.
Because it is extremely difficult for a creator to find

That its creation is not as it was expected, planned, moulded and shaped to be.

Everybody needs good neighbours

"Even the Queen relies on a good neighbour," my mother likes to say
And this is true within your homely classroom, too.
I am blessed with a fantastic teaching neighbour,
Frank and to the point
When teaching fractions as when discussing life,
Ready with an origami, chocolates or rooibos tea on my desk
And silly videos on my phone
When I've had a rubbish day,
Offering me breathing techniques and a shoulder to cry on,
Tips on classroom activities and stationery,
Some relationship and social life advice thrown in for good measure.
A classroom sisterhood,
Us teacher neighbours
Have got each other's back
Particularly when a dress' back button comes undone and we must stitch it back
Stealthily,
With five minutes to go before a lesson.

When We Made Amends

Who would have thought that teachers, too, would have lessons to learn?
That Miss Trunchbull and Miss Honey would,
After all that time,
Come to an understanding, a dialogue, an acceptance
Of each other's ways and vulnerabilities?
Miss Trunchbull's face has turned a calmer shade of pink,
Pastel and soothed,
No longer angry and mistrusting.
Miss Honey's voice is no longer trembling and fearful,
Feet planted solidly
On her classroom floor.
They even turn to each other for advice.
They even, occasionally, hug.
What would Matilda say, seeing this?

Proud

Today the sun was shining and I'd had a decent night's sleep,
So it was that little bit easier
For me to feel proud,
Like a Mother Duck with her brood of ducklings
Swimming in a neat row behind her.
Proud of those who truly exceeded my expectations
Making me do a double-take at the name on their book's cover,
Mouthing, "Is this really them?"
Proud of those who display independence
In finishing a task, in tying their shoelaces, in getting on with life without as much
guidance.
Proud of those who overcame their fears of failure,
Of loneliness, of new and unknown things
Of those whose penmanship was less scraggly and scribbled,
Of those who found their voice to speak a little louder,
To sing the higher notes in choir practice,
To expand a little wider when faced with unkindness and mean words.
It was that little bit easier
Feeling so proud
To write my class' reports today.

Inside Out

Inside brightly-coloured display boards
Surrounded by Match-Attack cards and unicorn stickers,
Children's lockers stream their contents
In the early morning bustle.

You are out and ask for a word,
Your eyes betray emotions which even your
Brave sparkly panther earrings
Cannot mask and protect.

You speak, ask for help, and cry
For things no teaching degree can explain or fix,
For things only humanity, love and compassion can aid,
I offer a tissue in lieu of a hug.

The bond between mother and son,
The strain of changed circumstances, new arrangements and old battles,
Mood swings, anger and affection
Are discussed as you turn your heart inside out.

I can only support from the inside, listen, observe,
Try and understand parenthood, divorce and everything in between.
Teacher, mentor and confidante in between,
With my own heart turned inside out.

Residential

44 pupils, 5 teachers, countless rucksacks, suitcases and holdalls;
2 precious first aid kits containing
Bundles of plastic bags for the coach journey ahead;
10 "Can I go to the toilet?" when we've only just set off,
3 "I don't like my sandwich filling,"
12 "I'm thirsty, Miss!"
8 are homesick on the first evening,,
A few too many who have forgotten to shower, for my liking.
6 days,
17 activities including climbing, go karting, team building, abseiling, forest skills,
Chanting round a fire, torchlight stories, hair braiding, caving, orienteering, treasure hunting.
A few tears for good measure, but not too many,
Lots more smiles and laughs, each day.
4 misplaced sweaters and roughly 11 caps,
9 "Where have you been?" and a few more "You're late!"
1 sunburn – there's always one…
7 lost room keys on checkout,
13 Cokes, teas and coffees consumed to keep us all going,
30 different colours of friendship bracelets knotted,
15 Fidget Spinners and Pokémon cards traded,
44 long hugs at our return to school,
1 long sleep in my own bed at the end of it all.
Another Leavers' residential trip,
Safely over.

Makeshift Family Album

July 5th. The last day of school. Yet again.
Giddiness, sunshine, corridors echoing with laughter and holiday plans,
Playdates scheduled already for three weeks from now.
A shy knock on the door;
You steel yourself, tissues ready, expecting this:
It's the Leavers.
Tall, so tall, how did they get so tall?
Awkwardly creeping over me, already in their puberty.
Their eagerness,
Their uncertainty of what is to come.
How did they grow up so quickly?
I swear I held that boy's hand not too long ago as he had grazed his knee playing football.
I swear that girl was discussing Disney films with me just last term.
I swear this was the class I labelled as 'the tricky one'.
Yet, here they are. Ready for the outside world.
Oh, are they though.
Yes, yes they are. Now more than ever
They don't say much, but hold out a card
And before I know it, they hold out their arms and yearbooks
I let them hug me, wishing to infuse confidence and street credibility into their hearts
Through some abstract process of osmosis
A snapshot for my own album
A makeshift family of sorts
Goodbye. Take care.
"Thank you, Miss. We loved your lessons."
I'm fine. I reach for the tissues. I'm fine.

Politics

I never quite understood politics and its ins and outs;
I must admit, it is a flaw of mine.
So I understand it even less when it comes to play
Within the staffroom walls and the school site.
Activities, power games and relationships
Among people who, quite frankly, have not been facing a group of wide-eyed children
In a classroom for quite some time
Continues to puzzle me,
In its jolting me out of my idealised, perhaps naïve, concept of teaching.
Supposedly, status should matter among us;
Reputation, competitiveness, organisation of a leadership structure,
Newspaper headlines,
Medium term plans,
Demonstration and tracking of pupil progress and improvement,
Entrance into grammar schools.
Before I know it, I've zoned out;
I must admit, it is a flaw of mine.
So I understand it even less when we come to have to demonstrate it.
I innocently thought I was here to… teach?
Entice curiosity?
Whereas I find myself in a… business? Discussing politics?
My history teachers would be decidedly amused.
Myself, less so.

In Miss Tablet's Lessons

Delivering lessons remotely to the
Same standard we would have in the classroom.
Easier said than done
In these scary times of The Virus,
Despite the technology available.
How do you replicate your tone of voice,
Your eyebrows' curves of reprimand and praise,
Your hand gestures when explaining and reading aloud
Through the screen of a tablet?
How do you keep children's eyes twinkling
And their foreheads from furrowing in worry
When you are not behind the safety of your desk
And the paper decorations aren't shadowing your classroom windows?
One can but try, with creativity and forethought
To distract, entice and entertain
Whilst the world outside resembles a dystopian novel
And you are left without answers to questions posed.

Perspectives (the Covid-19 edit)

I admit it. I hold my hands up.
I thought online learning was karma's darkly humorous way
Of allowing parents to truly understand
Our perspective.
'Now they will know what it's really like,' I thought,
'How much hard work it can really be,
Which of their children really listens,
Which ones are truly talented and dedicated
And which ones are not.'
I prepared myself for plaintive e-mails and unnecessary questions, too.

I also admit it. I hold my hands up.
I have not received a single one of those.
What I have received instead
Are gifts, thoughtful messages, from children and parents alike,
Asking after my family,
Giving me advice on where to stock up on essentials (like vodka),
Telling me my bits of work have made the children's hearts soar.
Telling me to please, keep safe.

I admit this, too. I hold my hands and my tissues up.
I have been crying in front of my computer screen,
Crying at the sudden change
Of perspectives.

Seesaw

These days of forced seclusion have my mood swinging up and down
So much that my boyfriend must be nostalgic of my PMS.
As I'm trying to get to grips with online learning tools
Content, learning, communication – all while remaining positive –
Is harder to balance than a spring loaded seesaw in a playground.
First, we must allow the pupils a break
Encourage yoga! Mud kitchens! Tree climbing! Crafts by their sofas!
Then the seesaw tilts again.
More spellings! Find a way to test them! Give feedback! More!
No time to settle and take it in as, once more, it shifts and creaks,
Leaning over the other direction.
This is too much! Parents cannot handle it! Reign it in! Don't make it more stressful!
Meanwhile your Disney jigsaw is strewn across your notes,
You've had 5 different snacks and you watch the clock creep to lunchtime.
You've had a little cry, a laugh, and then a bigger cry,
You've scraped your hair back, meaning serious business,
You've prepared to adjust your CV to include crisis management
And all that it entails.

Actually, at Home

Behind classroom doors
We hear stories of birthday parties
And of numerous friends and family visiting
While actually, at home it's just you and your mum
And your imaginary Husky.

Behind classroom doors
You boast stories of girlfriends
And selfies, friend requests and Direct Messages
While actually, at home it's lots of staring at the mirror
Wondering who it is you really fancy, and why, and who you can ask this.

Behind classroom doors
You brag about your newest toys, video games
And adventurous holidays
While actually, at home it's just wishes of somebody to play with
And splash around with, away from phones, PCs and virtual meetings.

Very often, we can see what you conceal
Behind classroom doors
Within your vulnerable, young hearts,
In your confused, craving minds,
Despite of what we hear you say.

The Teachers and the Sea

Captaining the ship
Through both rough and calm waters,
We steer through your references
To the latest hits and YouTube clips,
Past cartoons, trends, and online games.
You young sailors
Keep a lookout
Announcing the latest slang
From the weather-beaten crow's nest.
We discipline and instruct the crew
Who navigates and musters social media platforms
With a simple click, and no chartered maps.
We may be your captains
Yet, in times like these,
What your fresh minds can show us
Is vaster than any of the maritime coordinates.

Connection Problems

We are back where we started from, almost a year from now
Teaching from our bedrooms and kitchens,
Whilst eager children who have ditched uniforms for onesies and pyjamas
Await instructions from their screens.

We encounter the dreaded connection problems
That stop us from projecting, file sharing, editing and scribbling live,
That stop them from accessing, listening, asking, catching up
Scuppering and marring our mutual efforts.

Online learning allows us to contact IT Departments
When connection problems arise now
They can sort, fix and recalibrate remotely
Without our direct involvement,
But what will happen a few weeks and months from now,
When we return to classrooms in person
And other types of connection problems arise?

The Reason

I sometimes do wonder
In days so frenetic and fraught
Of tears, sniffles, lost lunchboxes and unfinished worksheets
About the Reason behind
What I prepare, think, do and say.

The Reason behind the sleepless nights,
The worries, the book piles,
The emails, the lack of a 9-5 structure, the loss
Some nights
Of the person I am, the core, the fulcrum.

The Reason, like a Grail or a rune or a rainbow's end,
Lies behind smiles, confidence, and a hand held with
Nonchalance.
Behind completed quests towards comprehension answers
and Reading Records and extended writing tasks and grammar quizzes.
Behind cards of thanks and chocolate boxes.
Behind phrases and sentences you wish to collect in a quote book.
Behind goodbyes and sighs for the end of a school day
Behind excited hellos and curious oval mouths moved by surprise.
The Reason for my job
And for much more than just my job
Lies within all this.

TABLE OF CONTENTS

Foreword 9
Now I know my ABCs 11
Close Encounters of the After School Kind 13
Never Enough 14
Ones of Your Own 15
Fleeing the Nest 16
Learning Curves 17
Assembly 18
Another Year Over 19
Miss Honey and Miss Trunchbull 20
Parents Evening Jousting 21
Pastoral Care 22
The Show Must Go On 23
Perspectives 24
Technological Proximity 25
Through Readers' Eyes 27
Leaving Their Mark 28
Visitors to the Zoo 29
Vitamin C 30
Festive Outlook on Life 31
(Not) Fitting a Mould 32
Everybody needs good neighbours 34
When We Made Amends 35
Proud 36
Inside Out 37
Residential 38
Makeshift Family Album 39
Politics 40
In Miss Tablet's Lessons 41
Perspectives (the Covid-19 edit) 42
Seesaw 43

Actually, at Home 44
The Teachers and the Sea 45
Connection Problems 46
The Reason 47

www.ingramcontent.com/pod-product-compliance
Lightning Source LLC
LaVergne TN
LVHW092100060526
838201LV00047B/1482